W9-CBY-332

The Moonstone

BY WILKIE COLLINS

Abridged and adapted by CARLI LAKLAN

Illustrated by MEREDITH BROOKS

 A PACEMAKER CLASSIC

Fearon Education
a division of
PITMAN LEARNING, INC.
Belmont, California

PACEMAKER CLASSICS

Robinson Crusoe
The Moonstone
The Jungle Book
The Last of the Mohicans
Treasure Island
Two Years Before the Mast
20,000 Leagues Under the Sea
Tale of Two Cities

ISBN-0-8224-9220-2

Library of Congress Catalog Card Number: 67-25786

Printed in the United States of America.

Contents

1 Mr. Franklin's Story

My name is Betteredge. I have a story to tell. It is a strange story. It makes me afraid even to think about it. But I must tell it.

I lived in England in 1848. I worked for Lady Verinder. She lived in a big house by the sea. She had a daughter named Rachel.

Miss Rachel was a very pretty girl and people liked her. But bad things were going to happen to her, very bad things.

A big party was being planned on Saturday for Miss Rachel's birthday. Dr. Candy, an old family friend, was asked to come. Tall Mr. Godfrey Ablewhite was asked. His sisters were coming too. So were nice Mr. Franklin Blake and many other people. It was to be a happy time.

I worked hard to get everything ready. I had the big house cleaned. I told the cook to get the food ready. I got flowers from the garden.

I was tired. So, I thought I would rest. I went out to sit in the sun. But I heard a strange sound. I could not tell what it was. But it came from the garden.

I went to look in the garden. I saw three men there. They had dark skin and dark eyes.

They had on strange white clothes. They were not at all like our English clothes. A small boy was with them. They were looking at the house.

"What do you want?" I asked.

"We would like to do tricks at the party," one of the men said.

How they knew we were going to have a party, I could not tell. But I did not like their looks. I told them to go.

They started to leave. I hid behind a tree and watched them. I saw them stop on the road. Then I saw something very strange. The men turned back to look at the house. For a long time they looked at it. They had a funny look on their faces. It made me afraid.

The men turned to the small boy. They told him to hold out his hand. He did not want to. He looked afraid. But the men made him put out his hand.

One of the men put something black into the boy's hand. Then he put his hand on the boy's head. The man made a sign in the air.

The boy stood as though he were made of stone. He began to talk in a funny way. "I see the Englishman," he said. "He is coming. He is on the road."

What was he talking about? Who was coming? Who was on the road? I could not make a thing out of what the boy said.

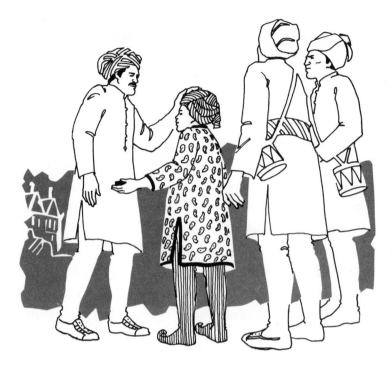

The three men moved close to the boy. They gave him a hard look. The boy looked more afraid.

"Does he have it with him?" the men asked.

"Yes," the boy said.

"Good!" the men cried. "Will he come toda⁻'?"

"I do not know," the boy said.

The men tried to make the boy say more. But the boy said nothing. One of the men made another sign in the air. He blew into the boy's face. The boy moved and opened his eyes. Then, taking the boy with them, the men went down the road.

3

What could it all have been about? I did not know. But I did not like any part of what I had seen and heard.

I went back to the house. The cook came out of the house as I came to the back door. She told me that Rosanna, one of the servants, had left her work. She had gone for a walk!

What was going on, I wondered.

I went to get Rosanna. I knew she would be on the beach near our house.

There was a strange place on the beach. It was called The Shivering Sand. It was quicksand. If you stepped on it you went down—down—down under the sand. You never came up. Anything placed on the quicksand went down the same way.

People were afraid of this place. No children played near it. No animals went there. Even birds did not fly near it. But Rosanna always went there. She liked to look at The Shivering Sand.

She was a strange girl. She had once been a thief. She took many things that did not belong to her. A policeman caught her and put her in jail.

When she got out of jail, Rachel's mother let her work at our house. Rosanna did her work well. She did nothing bad. But the other servants in the house did not like her.

I found Rosanna just where I had thought she would be. She was on the beach, looking at The Shivering Sand.

"Why do you come to this place?" I asked.

"I can not help it," she said in a strange voice. "I have to come here."

"You must not say such things," I told her.

But she did not listen to me. She just looked at The Shivering Sand. It was as though she could not take her eyes away from it.

"It looks as if there are many people under the quicksand," she said. "It looks as if they are trying to get out. But they can not. They just go down—down—down."

I had heard enough of such wild talk. I was about to tell Rosanna to go back to the house at once. But just then I heard my name called.

Rosanna turned. Her eyes opened wide. Her face grew red.

I turned to see who was coming. It was Mr. Franklin. I was surprised to see him. He had come down from London early.

"Hello," I called. "I thought you were not coming until this afternoon."

"I made new plans," he said. "I took an early train."

As he came up to us, Rosanna made a strange sound. She looked at Mr. Franklin with wide eyes. Then she got up and ran.

5

"What a strange girl," Mr. Franklin said. "What is the matter with her?"

"I don't know," I said. "She is one of the servants at the house. How are you, Mr. Franklin? I am glad to see you."

"Thank you, Betteredge," he said.

He did not look happy. "What is the matter?" I asked.

He looked all around as if he were afraid someone would hear him.

"Betteredge," he said, stepping close to me. "I have brought a present for Miss Rachel. It is a diamond, a very big diamond."

"I should think that would make you happy," I said.

"The diamond is bad luck," he said. "Let me tell you the story of this diamond. Then you will see why it is bad luck.

"Many years ago the diamond belonged to people in India. They were called Hindoos. They believed in a god called the Moon God. They made a statue of the Moon God. It had a big diamond set between its eyes. The diamond was called the Moonstone. No one was ever to take the Moonstone.

"But bad times came to the Hindoos. Soldiers came to their country. The soldiers set fire to houses and took everything they could get their hands on. The only thing the Hindoos saved was their statue of the Moon God.

"In the dark of night the Hindoos carried the statue to a city called Benares. There they put up a beautiful building of gold for the statue. Over the door they put these words:

Let no man take the Moonstone.
Bad luck will come to him who does.

"Many years went by. The Hindoos watched over the Moonstone. But then the English soldiers came to India. There was a great battle and the Hindoos lost. After the battle, many buildings were set on fire. Many things were

7

taken. And one thing that was taken was the Moonstone.

"The Hindoos could not get it back. But they sent men to be near it, no matter where it was. And the words over the door were true. Every man or woman who owned the diamond had very bad luck.

"The Hindoos said that some day they would get their diamond back. They said they would do anything to get it. They would even kill."

Mr. Franklin had finished his story. He took a box from his pocket and opened it.

"Look," he said. "This is the diamond."

I had never seen anything like it. It was almost as big as an egg. It seemed as bright as the sun. But there was something very strange about it. Beautiful as it was, it made me afraid.

"Why did you bring it to Miss Rachel?" I asked.

"I had to," Mr. Franklin said. He moved close to my side. "Betteredge," he said, "the English soldier who took the diamond was Miss Rachel's uncle."

My mouth fell open. "I knew he was a bad man," I said. "Rachel's mother would not let him come to the house. But I did not know he had ever done anything this bad."

"Yes," said Mr. Franklin. "He took the diamond. The Hindoos tried to get it back. They even tried to kill him to get it. But he put the diamond in a bank. They could never get it out."

"But why are you bringing it to Miss Rachel now?" I asked.

"Her uncle has died," Mr. Franklin said. "He left the diamond to Miss Rachel."

"But he knew it was bad luck," I said. "Did he want to give bad luck to Miss Rachel?"

"I don't know," said Mr. Franklin.

"Are you going to give her the diamond?" I asked.

Mr. Franklin looked sad. He loved Miss Rachel. He did not want to bring her bad luck.

"I must give it to her," he said. "The diamond would bring over $300,000. It is hers now."

"It may be that the Hindoos do not know where the diamond is," I said. Then I thought of the three strange men who had been in the garden. I told Mr. Franklin about them. I told him how they had talked about "it."

"They were talking about the diamond," he said. "They must be Hindoos. They found out I was bringing it here."

"Then they will come back for it!" I cried.

What should we do? We thought and thought. "Mr. Franklin," I said, "you must take the diamond to town. Put it in the bank. Leave it there until the day of the birthday party."

"I will do so at once," he said.

As I watched Mr. Franklin ride off to town, I wondered. Will he make it? Will he get to town with the diamond? Or will the Hindoos catch him?

2 The Birthday Party

I left the garden and went into the kitchen. The cook called me to her.

"You must do something about Rosanna," she said.

"What has she done now?" I asked.

"She thinks she is in love with Mr. Franklin," the cook said.

My mouth fell open. "How can she think such a thing?" I cried. "She has only seen Mr. Franklin once—just a few minutes ago."

"That does not matter," the cook said. "She thinks she is in love with him."

"Go back to your work," I said. "I don't want to hear one more word about such things. I have enough to think about."

I tried to do my own work. But I kept looking out the window for the Hindoos. I wondered if Mr. Franklin was all right.

At last I saw him coming back. I ran out to meet him. "Did you get the diamond to the bank?" I asked.

"Yes, I did," he said. "I did not set eyes on the Hindoos."

"That makes me feel better," I said.

"Keep watch, Betteredge," Mr. Franklin said.

"If you see the Hindoos near the house, let me know."

"I will, Mr. Franklin," I answered.

Then Mr. Franklin went into the house to see Miss Rachel. She was very happy to see him. For the next two days they had a good time together. I knew Mr. Franklin was in love with her. And I was sure she was falling in love with him.

"They will get married before long!" I said to the cook one day.

Rosanna was in the kitchen, too. She began to cry and ran to her room.

"See!" the cook said. "I told you! She is in love with him!"

"It will do her no good," I said. "Mr. Franklin loves Miss Rachel."

At last the day of the party came. Mr. Franklin got ready to go to town for the diamond.

"Be careful, Mr. Franklin," I said.

"I will be," he said as he rode off.

I had a lot of work to do. I tried not to think about Mr. Franklin and the diamond. But I could not help thinking about it. What if the Hindoos knew he was bringing the diamond back? Would they kill him to get it?

I was very glad when at last I saw him coming back. He was not alone. Mr. Godfrey and his two sisters were with him. They had come from their homes in London. Mr. Godfrey was a lawyer.

"I did not see the Hindoos," Mr. Franklin told me. If they find out that the diamond is back here . . . !"

He took the diamond to Miss Rachel and gave it to her. Her eyes grew big.

"It is beautiful!" she cried. "Look how bright it is!"

She put it on her dress. I wished she would put it away where no one could see it. All I could think of was that it was bad luck. But Miss Rachel did not know that. Mr. Franklin had not told her the story of the diamond. He did not want Miss Rachel to be afraid.

The other people who came to the party all talked about the diamond. "How beautiful it is!" they all cried. But one man, Mr. Murthwaite, had other thoughts. He had been all over the world. So he knew a lot about many countries.

"Miss Rachel," he said, "if you ever go to India, don't take that diamond."

"Why?" she asked.

"There are men there who might kill you for it," he said.

I looked at him. Did he know the story of the diamond? Did he know it was bad luck?

The party should have been a happy one. But nothing seemed to go right. Mr. Godfrey did not talk. Mr. Franklin talked too much. At one point, he was talking to Dr. Candy.

"Dr. Candy," he said, "I don't think that medicine helps people very much."

"I could show you how much help it is!" Dr. Candy cried.

"How?" Mr. Franklin said.

"You have not been sleeping well, have you?" Dr. Candy asked.

"No, I have not been," answered Mr. Franklin.

"I could give you medicine that would make you sleep," Dr. Candy said. "It would be a deep sleep, not like any you ever had before."

Mr. Franklin laughed. He started to say something. But just then, I looked out the window. What I saw made me cry out. There in the garden were the three Hindoos and the boy! I hurried to the door to send them away. But Mr. Godfrey's sisters had seen them, too.

"They do tricks!" one of the girls cried. "Let's ask them to do some!"

Before I could stop them, they had run to the door. All the others followed. Miss Rachel was with them. And there, on her dress, was the diamond for the Hindoos to see!

"What shall we do?" I asked Mr. Franklin.

"Quick!" he said. "Stand on one side of Miss Rachel. I will stand on the other side. If the Hindoos try anything, we will be ready."

We took our places. The Hindoos did their tricks. At any minute they might try to get the diamond. I saw one of them looking at Miss Rachel. I stepped in front of her.

Just then, Mr. Murthwaite went up to the Hindoos. He said something to them that I could not hear. The Hindoos looked afraid. They stopped their tricks and went away in a hurry.

"That is too bad!" Miss Rachel cried. "They were fun." Then she and her friends went back into the house.

Mr. Murthwaite kept Mr. Franklin and me

in the garden. "Those Hindoos are not what they seem to be," he said. "They are only making believe that they do tricks for a living."

"How do you know?" Mr. Franklin asked.

"I have been to India," he said. "I am sure those three men are Brahmans."

"What are Brahmans?" I asked.

"They are very high Hindoos," he said. "They should never leave their country. If they do, they give up all their rights. And they can never get them back. It must be a very great thing that made them come here."

"The diamond!" I cried. "It is the Moonstone. It is the diamond that was taken from the Hindoos' Moon God."

"I thought so," Mr. Murthwaite said. "I must tell you, the Hindoos will get that diamond. They will not go back to India without it."

He looked at Mr. Franklin. "The Hindoos knew you were bringing the diamond from London," he said. "I am surprised they did not try to get if from you on the way."

"I left some time before I had planned to," Mr. Franklin said.

"A good thing you did," said Mr. Murthwaite. "They would have killed you if they found you alone."

"Will the Hindoos come back soon?" I asked.

"I don't think so," said Mr. Murthwaite. "They

know I am on to them. I think they will wait for another time. But be careful."

At last the party was over. The friends who lived near went home. Mr. Franklin and Mr. Godfrey and his sisters were staying at our house. Miss Rachel was saying good night to them.

"Where are you going to put your diamond?" her mother asked.

"In the cabinet in the sitting room next to my bedroom," Miss Rachel said.

"That is not a good place!" said Lady Verinder. "There is no lock on the cabinet."

Miss Rachel laughed. "Mother!" she said. "You don't think anyone in this house would take my diamond, do you?"

I wanted to say that a thief might break into the house in the night. But a look from Mr. Franklin stopped me. He did not want Miss Rachel to be afraid.

Miss Rachel and Lady Verinder went to their rooms.

"Want to have a drink before you go to bed, Franklin?" Mr. Godfrey asked.

"All right," said Mr. Franklin.

"Go on up to your room," Mr. Godfrey said. "I'll bring the drinks."

I went through the house and locked all the doors and windows. No one can get in now, I thought.

3 Where Is the Diamond?

I woke up at about seven the next morning. I had just finished dressing when a servant girl knocked on my door.

"Come at once!" she cried. "The diamond is gone!"

For a minute I could not move. Then I ran from my room and up to Miss Rachel's sitting room. She was standing by the door. Her face was white.

"Is it true, Miss Rachel?" I cried. "Is the diamond gone?"

She did not say a word.

I looked at the cabinet. The doors were open. I hurried to look. The diamond was not there.

"Miss Rachel put the diamond there last night," the servant girl said. "I saw her."

"You are sure you put it there, Miss Rachel?" I asked.

She had a strange look on her face. She looked at me. But she did not seem to see me.

"The diamond is gone," she said in a strange voice. Then, without another word, she went into her bedroom and shut the door.

Mr. Godfrey hurried in. "What is this I have heard?" he asked. "Is the diamond gone?"

"Yes, Mr. Godfrey, it is," I answered.

"Who could have taken it?" he asked. "Do you think one of the servants...?"

Before I could say anything, Mr. Franklin came in. He looked as if he did not feel very well. "I had a good night's sleep," he said. "But I still feel heavy headed."

"I'll get you something hot to drink," I said. I sent the servant girl to get it.

Lady Verinder came hurrying in. "What is going on?" she asked. I told her the bad news.

"Oh, no!" she cried. "I was afraid something like this would happen." She went into Miss Rachel's room.

I gave Mr. Franklin the hot drink. He felt better at once. "Look all around the room," he said. "We must be sure the diamond is not here."

We looked, but we could not find the diamond. "Betteredge," said Mr. Franklin, "go around to all the windows and doors. See if they are still locked."

I hurried to do as he asked. I went all through the house. All the doors and windows were still locked. How could anyone have come in?

Lady Verinder came back into the sitting room. "I don't know what to do," she said. "This has been too much for Rachel. She just lies there on her bed. She will not say a word about the diamond, not even to me. We must get a policeman. There is nothing else we can do."

"I will go," said Mr. Franklin. "And the first thing I am going to tell them is to find the Hindoos."

"What do you mean?" asked Mr. Godfrey.

"I don't have time to tell you now," Mr. Franklin said. "Wait until I get back. Then I will tell you and Lady Verinder the story. But I am sure the Hindoos took the diamond."

I went with Mr. Franklin as he got his horse. "How did the Hindoos get into the house?" I asked.

"One of them must have come into the house. He could have come in while we were having the party," he said. "He hid until we were all asleep. Then he took the diamond and left by the front door. It locked behind him."

"That must be what happened," I said as Mr. Franklin rode off. Who else would have taken the diamond?

All that morning, the servants could talk about nothing but the diamond. Miss Rachel stayed in her room. Mr. Godfrey did not know what he wanted to do. One minute he said he was going back to London. The next minute he said that he would stay. It was a hard day for all of us.

It was early in the afternoon when Mr. Franklin came back. "A policeman, Superintendent Seegrave, will be here soon," he said.

"What about the Hindoos, Mr. Franklin?" I asked.

"The Hindoos did not take the diamond," he said.

I could not believe my ears. "Why do you say that?" I cried.

"They were seen coming back to town. It was right after we sent them away from the party," Mr. Franklin said. "They were in town all night. Even so, Superintendent Seegrave put them in jail. He wants to be sure they are out of the way."

"Good," I said. It made me feel better to know they were in jail.

Mr. Franklin went to tell Rachel's mother and Mr. Godfrey the story of the Moonstone.

Soon Superintendent Seegrave came to the house. There was another policeman with him.

"Someone in this house took the diamond," the Superintendent said to me. He told the other policeman to keep the servants together. He wanted to keep them from going to their rooms. "Take me to Miss Rachel's sitting room," he said.

21

I did as he asked. "Be careful of the door," I said. "It was painted. The paint still may be wet."

The Superintendent began looking around the room. All at once, the servants came running into the sitting room. "Why keep us out of our rooms?" they cried. "Do you think one of us took the diamond?"

"Go back to your work," Superintendent Seegrave said. "Look what one of you has just done!"

He pointed to the fresh paint on the door. There was a spot on it. "One of your dresses did that!" he said. "Now go back to the kitchen and stay there."

He asked to see Miss Rachel. But she would not come out of her room. Then all at once she opened the door and came out. "Where is Mr. Franklin?" she asked me.

I told her he was in the garden. Without another word, she went to the garden. I looked out the window. I could see the garden from it. I could not hear what she said. But she looked angry.

Mr. Franklin looked as though he could not believe what Miss Rachel was saying. Then Miss Rachel ran back into the house.

Superintendent Seegrave tried to talk to her.

"I do not want to talk to you!" she cried. "*I*

did not send for you! *I* don't want you here! My diamond is gone. You will never find it! No one will find it!"

She ran into her room and locked the door. We could hear her crying.

"Poor girl," I said. "This is a hard time for her."

"Betteredge," Superintendent Seegrave said. "Tell me about the servants."

"They are all good people," I said. I did not tell him Rosanna had been a thief. I did not think she would take the diamond. But who did?

"Take me to each servant's room," Superintendent Seegrave said. I did as he asked. He looked in each room. But he did not find the diamond. Then Superintendent Seegrave and the other policeman left. They went back to town.

Where could the diamond be? I was trying to think of an answer when Mr. Franklin sent for me. I went to the living room. Just as I was about to knock, the door opened. Rosanna came out. Her face grew red when she saw me. She ran to the kitchen. I wondered what she had been up to.

I went in to see Mr. Franklin. "Betteredge," he said, "I'm going to send to London for a policeman named Mr. Cuff. He is a very good policeman. I think he will find the diamond for us."

"I am glad to hear that, Mr. Franklin," I said. I started to leave the room.

Mr. Franklin stopped me. "There is something else I want to tell you," he said. "It is about Rosanna. I think she knows something about the diamond."

"Why do you think that?" I asked.

"She was just in here," he said. "She brought a ring I had dropped on the floor of my bedroom. I thanked her. I thought she would go then. But she did not. She looked at me in a strange way. Then she said, 'They will never find the diamond, will they?'

"Before I could answer, she said, 'They will never find who took it. *I* will see to that!' Then she heard you in the hall and ran out."

I did not tell Mr. Franklin that Rosanna thought she was in love with him. I was sure she was just trying to get him to think about her. "Mr. Franklin," I said, "I don't think Rosanna knows a thing about the diamond."

"Watch what she does just the same," he said. Then Mr. Franklin went out. He rode off to town to send word to Mr. Cuff in London.

I went into the kitchen. I was going to talk to Rosanna, but she was not there. I asked the cook where Rosanna was.

"She said she was sick. Then she went to her room," the cook told me.

That was funny. She had not looked sick a few minutes ago. It seemed very strange to me.

But I did not believe that Rosanna had taken the diamond. I was sure the Hindoos had taken it.

In two days, Mr. Cuff came. He went right to work. First he looked at the room from which the diamond had been taken.

He saw the spot on the paint on the door. "How did that happen?" he asked.

"One of the servants did it with her dress," I said.

"Which servant did it?" he asked, looking at me.

"What does it matter?" I answered.

"It matters," said Mr. Cuff. "What time were the servants in this room?"

"Ten in the morning," I said.

"And when was the door painted?" he asked.

"The day before the diamond was taken," I told him.

"How long does the paint take to dry?" he asked.

"Not very long," Mr. Franklin said. "The paint should have been dry the next morning."

"So the spot on the paint was not made by a servant's dress," Mr. Cuff said. "It was made the night the diamond was taken. The spot was made by the one who took the diamond. There will be paint on his clothes."

All at once, Rachel ran out of her bedroom. "I will tell you something!" she cried. "Look for the diamond if you must! But do not let Mr. Franklin help you!"

With that she went back into her room. Mr. Franklin looked as if he had been hit in the face. He turned to Mr. Cuff. "Can you find out who took the diamond?" he asked.

And then Mr. Cuff said a surprising thing!

"No one took the diamond!" he said.

Our mouths fell open. "But it is gone!" I cried.

Mr. Cuff smiled. "Just wait," he said. "You will see."

4 Following Rosanna

"I want to look at all the clothes in the house," said Mr. Cuff. "I want to find out if any clothes have paint on them."

But Miss Rachel would not let him look at her clothes.

"Then I do not want to look at any of them," Mr. Cuff said. "I must see *all* the clothes in the house. If I can not, I do not want to see any."

He would say no more than that. Just then, Rosanna went down the hall.

"How long has she worked here?" Mr. Cuff asked me.

"Why do you ask?" I said.

"Because the last time I saw her, she was in jail," he said.

"Well, she has been good here," I told him.

"I wonder," he said in a hard voice. Then he walked off.

I felt as though nothing in the house would ever be right again.

Mr. Godfrey and his sisters left for London that afternoon. They seemed glad to be leaving.

Mr. Franklin stayed with us. He was very sad. Miss Rachel would not talk to him. She would not tell him why. Rosanna kept trying to talk to him all the time. But he did not want to talk to Rosanna.

In a few days, the Hindoos were let out of jail. I did not know where they went after they left jail. But they did not come to our house.

One day Mr. Cuff called Rosanna into the living room. He talked to her alone. Her face was white when she came out. Mr. Cuff did not tell me what they had talked about. He just said to let him know if Rosanna asked to leave the house.

A few minutes after that the cook called me into the kitchen. She told me that Rosanna wanted to go for a walk.

"She is up to something," said the cook. "She told me she was sick the other day. But she was not sick. In the afternoon, I went to her room to see her. Her door was locked. But she was not in her room."

"Where did she go?" I asked.

"The boy who brings the milk said he saw her that afternoon. She was walking to town," the cook said.

"Why would she say she was sick and then go to town?" I asked.

"I don't know," said the cook. "But I do know she locked herself in her room after supper. She would not let any of us in. She is up to no good!"

"That is enough!" I said. I ran to tell Mr. Cuff that Rosanna had gone for a walk.

"We will follow her," said Mr. Cuff. So, we hurried out the door after Rosanna.

Rosanna walked fast. She looked back now and then. But we did not let her see us.

She went to a small house on the beach. A friend of hers lived there. Her friend was called Limping Lucy.

Mr. Cuff and I hid behind some trees. We waited a long time. At last Rosanna came out of the house. She was hiding something under her coat. She started for The Shivering Sand.

"Shall we follow her?" I asked.

"No, there is nothing to hide behind," Mr. Cuff said. "She would see us."

"Do you think she is hiding the diamond under her coat?" I asked.

29

"No," said Mr. Cuff. "I think she is helping the one who does have the diamond."

"Who is that?" I asked.

"I can not tell you now," he said. "But you know what I said. The diamond has *not* been stolen."

I could not make heads or tails out of that. The diamond was gone. But Mr. Cuff said it had not been stolen! What kind of talk was this?

"Did you know Rosanna went to town the other day?" I asked.

"Yes," he said. "Don't you know why?"

"No," I said.

"She went to buy some cloth."

"Why?" I asked.

"Because she is the one who got paint on her clothes. She got it on her dress, I think."

"Then she was in the room the night the diamond was stolen!" I said.

"I think so," he said. "I think she went there and got paint on her dress. Then she learned I was looking for clothes with paint on them. So, she went to a store in town and got some cloth. Then she came home and locked herself in her room. She sat up all night making a new dress. Now she is going to throw the dress with the paint on it away. I think she is going to throw it into The Shivering Sand."

"Why don't you stop her?" I asked.

"I don't want her to know I am on to her," Mr. Cuff said. "Through her, I will catch the one who has the diamond."

I wanted to know more. But he would not tell me. "Come," he said. "We will go to Limping Lucy's house. I want to know what Rosanna did there."

We went to the house. Limping Lucy's mother let us in.

"Tell me what Rosanna did while she was here," Mr. Cuff said.

"She wrote a long letter," Lucy's mother said. "Then she asked me to give her a box. She wanted a piece of rope, too."

"Why did she want them?" I asked.

"She wanted the box to put some of her things in," said Lucy's mother. "The rope was to tie up her trunk. She is leaving your house."

"Leaving!" I said. "She did not tell me."

"That is what she told me," Lucy's mother said.

Mr. Cuff and I left the house.

"I wonder why Rosanna wants the box and rope?" he said.

"You were just told why," I said.

"No! No!" he said. "That is not why."

"Then what is she going to do with them?" I asked.

"I think she is going to put something in the box." Mr. Cuff said. She will tie the rope around the box. Then she will put the box down in The Shivering Sand. She will tie the other end of the rope to a rock. When she wants the box back, she will pull it up by the rope." He looked at me. "But what is she going to put in the box?" he asked.

"Her dress with the paint on it," I said.

"But why put it in the box?" he asked. "She could just throw it in The Shivering Sand. It would go down. It would never come back up. No, Betteredge. She is going to put something else in that box. It will be something she wants back. What would that be?"

"The diamond!" I cried.

"No!" he said. "She does not have the diamond. I am sure of that. It *must* be the dress with the paint on it. But I don't know why she wants to put it in the box."

"We could find the rope," I said. "We could pull the box up and open it. Then we could see what is in it."

"No," said Mr. Cuff. "She will have tied the rope where we could not find it. Come Betteredge. Let's go back to the house. I think something is about to happen."

We went back to the house. In the kitchen, the cook told us Rosanna had been home about

30 minutes. "And Lady Verinder wants to see you," she said to us.

We went up to Lady Verinder's room. "I must tell you something," said Lady Verinder. "Rachel is going away tomorrow. She is going to stay with her Aunt Elizabeth."

"When did she say that?" Mr. Cuff asked.

"About 30 minutes ago," Lady Verinder said.

About 30 minutes ago! Just after Rosanna came back from The Shivering Sand! Something was going on, all right.

Mr. Cuff told Lady Verinder he had to go to town in the morning. "Please keep Rachel here until I get back," he said.

"Can you tell me why?" Lady Verinder asked.

"Not now," Mr. Cuff said. "But she must stay until I get back. I must talk to her."

We left the room. I turned to Mr. Cuff. "You know something about Miss Rachel!" I cried. "You think she took her own diamond!"

"That is what she has done," he said.

"She would never do that!" I cried.

"Miss Rachel had the diamond all the time," he said. "And she told Rosanna that she has it."

"Why would she tell Rosanna?" I asked.

"Because she knows Rosanna was a thief. She needs her help."

"I don't believe you!" I cried. I walked away from him as fast as I could.

As I started down the hall, the door to the living room opened. Rosanna ran out.

"What is the matter?" I asked.

"Let me alone!" she cried. She ran to her room.

Then Mr. Franklin came into the hall. "Did you see Rosanna?" he asked.

"Yes," I said. "What happened?"

"I think she was going to tell me something," he said. "I was sitting in the living room reading. She came into the room. She was very strange. She seemed to want to talk to me. But she did not say anything. So, I looked down at my book. Then she cried, 'You will look at your book. But you will not look at me!' Then she ran off."

I left the living room and went to Rosanna's room. I knocked on the door. Then I called to her. But she would not talk to me. So, I went back to the living room. I told Mr. Franklin that Rosanna would not come back.

By now it was time for bed. I was glad of it. It had been a hard day. I went through the house and locked all the doors. Then I went to my room. On the way, I saw Mr. Cuff. He was sitting in a chair in front of Miss Rachel's sitting room.

"What are you doing here?" I asked.

"I think Rosanna will go to Miss Rachel's room in the night. She will try to talk to Miss Rachel," he said. "I am here to stop her."

5 To See Miss Rachel

Nothing happened in the night. Rosanna did not try to see Miss Rachel. No one tried to get into the house. And no one tried to leave it.

The next morning, Mr. Cuff got ready to go. Before he left, he asked Mr. Franklin and me to come into the garden. When we got to the garden, he talked to us in a soft voice.

"Mr. Franklin," he said, "you have been keeping something from me."

"No, I have not," Mr. Franklin said.

"Rosanna has tried to talk to you, has she not?" Mr. Cuff asked.

"I have nothing to say," Mr. Franklin said.

Just then Rosanna came into the garden. She was looking for Mr. Franklin. She stopped when she saw us. Mr. Cuff made believe he did not see her.

In a loud voice he asked Mr. Franklin, "Do you love Rosanna?"

"I do not!" Mr. Franklin said in just as loud a voice.

With a cry, poor Rosanna ran into the house. Mr. Cuff gave Mr. Franklin a look. Then he left us and went to town.

As soon as he was gone, Mr. Franklin turned to me. "I did not want to hurt Rosanna that way," he said. "But I was afraid she was going to say something in front of Mr. Cuff. I wanted to stop her."

"I will tell Rosanna," I said. Then we both left the garden.

As soon as I had time, I went to find Rosanna. She was in the kitchen. Her face was white. She moved as if she were asleep. I tried to tell her that Mr. Franklin had not wanted to hurt her. But she did not seem to hear me.

"Rosanna," I said. "Something is the matter. Don't try to hide it. Tell us what it is."

"I will," she said.

"Will you tell me?" I asked.

"No."

"Will you tell Mr. Franklin?" I asked.

"Yes," she said.

"He has gone for a walk," I said.

"That does not matter," she said. "I will not try to talk to him."

This was strange talk. How could she tell him if she did not talk to him?

"Why don't you go and talk to Rachel's mother?" I said. "She will help you."

"I know a better way," she said.

I could not get another word out of her. She walked out of the kitchen. I looked to see what time it was. It was almost two. Soon Mr. Cuff would be back.

I went to the garden to wait for him. He came at last.

"What did you find out." I asked.

"Rosanna did buy some cloth in town," said Mr. Cuff. "She got enough to make a dress. I *must* find that box she hid in The Shivering Sand. I want to see what is in it."

Before he could say more, the carriage came to the front of the house. It was there to pick up Miss Rachel. She came out and got into the carriage.

Mr. Cuff ran up to her. "One minute!" he cried.

"What do you want?" she asked.

"I want to tell you this," he said. "If you go now, you will make it harder to get back your diamond. Will you stay?"

"No!" she said.

Mr. Franklin ran from the house. "Rachel!" he cried. "Let me say good-by to you!"

She did not even look at him. She told the man driving the carriage to hurry. He made the horses run.

Mr. Franklin turned and went back into the house. He looked very sad.

Mr. Cuff watched the carriage with Miss Rachel in it. "She has something with her," he said. "She has the Moonstone diamond!"

"I don't believe you!" I cried.

"You will see," Mr. Cuff said. "Come. I am going to talk to Rosanna."

But Rosanna was gone! She was not in her room. She was not to be found.

"She will not get away!" Mr. Cuff cried.

He called the servants together. He asked if any of them had seen Rosanna. The cook had a story to tell.

"The boy brought the milk about 12," said the cook. "Rosanna gave him a letter to mail. It was to her friend, Limping Lucy. The boy told her it would not get there until Monday. He asked her why she did not take it to Limping Lucy herself. He said it would just take a few minutes to walk over. But Rosanna made him take it. She told him she wanted it to go by mail. She said that she did not want Lucy to get it until Monday."

The cook finished her story. Just then, a boy who worked in the barn ran up to us. "I saw Rosanna going to The Shivering Sand!" he cried. "She was running!"

"Quick!" Mr. Cuff cried. "Show me the way!"

They ran off. The rest of us stayed in the house. The minutes went by. The sky was getting very dark. The wind began to blow. What was happening at The Shivering Sand, I wondered.

The boy came running back. "Mr. Cuff wants one of Rosanna's shoes," he said to me. "He wants you to bring it to The Shivering Sand."

I ran to Rosanna's room to get a shoe. Then the boy and I hurried to The Shivering Sand with it. It was raining now. The wind blew harder.

I saw Mr. Cuff standing next to The Shivering Sand. The look on his face made me afraid.

"Give me the shoe!" he cried.

I gave it to him. He set it in a footprint in the sand. It fit the footprint. And the footprint pointed to the quicksand. He found another footprint, and another. They all went

to the quicksand. No one went away from it. I began to shake.

"Oh, my God!" Mr. Cuff cried.

And then I knew! Rosanna had killed herself by jumping into The Shivering Sand. She had gone down—down—down. Down under the quicksand. She would never be seen again.

We did not talk as we went back to the house. The boy had run on before us. So, all the people at the house knew what had happened. The servants were crying.

"She did it because she loved Mr. Franklin," the cook said. "Poor girl! He would not even look at her. She could not stand it. So, she killed herself."

I knew Mr. Cuff did not believe this. He thought she had jumped into The Shivering Sand because of the diamond. He was sure she knew something about it.

"You made Rosanna do this!" said Lady Verinder to Mr. Cuff. "I want you to go away from this house at once."

"Not until I tell you what I think," Mr. Cuff said. "You asked me to find out about the diamond. Now I am ready to tell you."

"Very well," Lady Verinder said. "Tell me."

"I think Rosanna knew something about the diamond," said Mr. Cuff. "I think this made her so afraid that she killed herself."

"What did she know?" asked Lady Verinder.

"I can not tell you for sure," Mr. Cuff said. "But I know who can."

"You mean Rachel?" asked Lady Verinder.

"I do," Mr. Cuff said.

Lady Verinder's face went white. She looked at Mr. Cuff. "You think my daughter has the diamond," she said. "*I* do not think she has it. Why would she hide her own diamond?"

"I think she needs money," he said. "She made believe the diamond was taken. Then she could try to get money for it."

"I give my daughter money," Lady Verinder said. "If she needed more, she would ask me."

"I think Miss Rachel is in some kind of trouble. I think she needs a lot of money," Mr. Cuff said. "She does not want you to know."

"Rachel is not in trouble," said Lady Verinder.

"Are you sure?" Mr. Cuff asked. "Think what she has done. She would not talk to Superintendent Seegrave. She would not talk to Mr. Franklin or to me. We are the people who have tried to get back her diamond. But she does not want it found."

"I don't believe you," said Lady Verinder.

"I told Miss Rachel not to leave this house," said Mr. Cuff. "I told her that would make it harder to find the diamond. But she left."

That did look bad for Miss Rachel, I thought. But Mr. Cuff had more to say.

"Let's look at something else," said Mr. Cuff. "Miss Rachel needed someone to help her. Rosanna was just the one. Rosanna had been a thief. She knew where to get money for the diamond. Rachel made Rosanna help her."

"That is not so!" cried Lady Verinder.

"I will show you that it is!" Mr. Cuff said. "I am going to visit Miss Rachel at her Aunt Elizabeth's house. I am going to surprise Rachel with the news that Rosanna has killed herself. Rachel will give herself away. She will tell all she knows."

Lady Verinder stood up. "You are not going to see my daughter," she said. "But *I am.*"

Mr. Cuff did not like this. But there was nothing he could do. The carriage was brought to the front of the house. Mr. Cuff, Lady Verinder, and I went outside. Lady Verinder got into the carriage. She looked at Mr. Cuff.

"I will tell you what Rachel says," she said. "Even if it is bad, I will tell you.

Then, she rode off in the carriage. All we could do now was wait.

6 The News from London

Mr. Cuff and I went into the house. He went up to his room. I went with him. He began to put his clothes into his bag.

"Are you leaving?" I asked.

"I will be," he said.

This was the best thing I had heard for days!

"So!" I said. "You don't think Miss Rachel has the diamond after all."

"I think she has it," Mr. Cuff said. "But her mother will never tell me what Miss Rachel says. They will both hide the real story of the diamond."

I gave him a hard look. Then I walked out and left him.

In the afternoon, a boy brought a note from Rachel's mother. I read it to Mr. Cuff. It said:

"I told Rachel about Rosanna. She does not know why Rosanna killed herself. Rachel says she never talked to Rosanna. Rosanna did not go to Rachel's room the night the diamond was taken. Rachel says she does not need money. And she told me she does not have the diamond.

"But there is one thing Rachel would not tell me. I asked her if she knew who has taken the diamond. She began to cry and would not say one word."

There the note ended. I looked up at Mr. Cuff. He looked very angry.

"She knows who took the diamond," Mr. Cuff said.

I did not want to hear any more from him. "Are you ready to go?" I asked.

"Yes," he said. "But you will see me again."

"Why?" I asked.

"You have not heard the last of the diamond," he said. "You will need me again."

"I don't think so," I said. I did not know what had happened to the diamond. Rosanna might have taken it. The diamond might be at the bottom of The Shivering Sand. I did not know.

"I will tell you four things," Mr. Cuff said. "One, you will hear from Rosanna's friend, Limping Lucy," he said. "Two, you will hear from the Hindoos again. Three, you will hear from a man in London. This man lends money on things like the diamond." He looked at me. "Last," he said, "you will hear that Miss Rachel is going to live in London."

He wrote a name on a piece of paper. Then he gave it to me. The name was *Mr. Septimus Luker.*

44

"He is the man in London who lends money on jewels," he said. "Watch for his name."

The way he said it made me afraid. "Please go now," I said.

Mr. Cuff picked up his bag and left.

Mr. Franklin was the next to leave. He was not happy at all.

"Where will you go?" I asked.

"What does it matter? I may go to France," he said. "I don't care where I go now. Miss Rachel does not love me any more."

"Stay here," I said. "She will come back soon. She still loves you."

"No," he said. "She and her mother are going to live in London."

My mouth fell open. Mr. Cuff had said she would live in London. He was right!

I said good-by to Mr. Franklin, and he left.

Now all the people who had made this house happy were gone. Mr. Franklin, Mr. Godfrey, Miss Rachel and her mother—they had all gone away. And poor Rosanna had killed herself.

Two weeks ago this had been a happy house. Then the diamond had been brought here. And from that time, only bad things had happened.

The story of the Moonstone was true. It was bad luck.

What else would happen to us?

It was a week after Miss Rachel's birthday party. It rained all day that Sunday. Monday afternoon the sun came out.

I was in the garden. Who did I see coming down the road but Limping Lucy! Why would she come here now that Rosanna was gone?

I felt cold all over. Mr. Cuff had said I would hear from Limping Lucy. And here she was.

She looked like a wild thing. "Where is he?" she cried.

"Who?" I asked.

"That Mr. Franklin!" she said. "He killed Rosanna!"

"That is wild talk," I said. "Rosanna killed herself. You know that."

"But it was because of him!" she answered. Then she began to cry.

"Rosanna was my friend," she said. "She could not help falling in love with Mr. Franklin. But he would not even look at her. Where is he? I must see him."

"Why?" I asked.

"I have a letter for him," she said.

"From Rosanna?" I asked.

"Yes. It came this morning. It was with a letter Rosanna mailed to me. I must give it to him," she said.

"He is gone," I told her. "Give me the letter. I will mail it to Mr. Franklin."

Limping Lucy would not do that. "Rosanna said I must put it into his hands," she answered. "I will not give it to anyone else. If Mr. Franklin wants the letter, he will have to come back here. Then he can get it from me."

With those words, Limping Lucy left. What was in the letter? Was it about the Moonstone? Would we ever find out? Mr. Franklin might never come back.

In a few days, I got a letter from Lady Verinder. She told me to send the servants away. She said to close the house and come to London.

There was another letter in the mail, too. It was from Mr. Cuff. In it there was a news story cut out of a paper. It was about Mr. Septimus Luker, the man who lends money on jewels!

I read the story. Three Hindoos had come to his house. They told him they wanted to do tricks for him. He sent them away. But they came back. Mr. Luker called a policeman. He was afraid the Hindoos wanted to take something from him. He did not say what he thought they would take.

I put the paper down. I was afraid. Mr. Cuff had told me that these four things would happen. Now all of them *had* happened.

Miss Rachel was in London. And the Hindoos were there. They were trying to take something from Mr. Luker. Was it the diamond? Who could have taken it to him? Was it Miss Rachel?

48

7 Two Strange Stories

I went to London soon after I got Lady Verinder's letter. Lady Verinder and Miss Rachel had a very nice house there. But something was the matter. Miss Rachel laughed a lot. She went to parties. She made believe she was having a good time. But she did not look happy.

Mr. Godfrey came to see her quite often. She will never like him as much as she did Mr. Franklin, I thought.

One day we saw something in the paper about Mr. Godfrey. A strange thing had happened to him.

Mr. Godfrey had been to his bank to get money. He had only been home a few minutes when a boy brought him a note. The boy said an old lady had asked him to bring it.

Mr. Godfrey read the note. "Come to 25 North Street," it said. "I want to give you some money for the Children's Aid Society."

Mr. Godfrey was not surprised. He often helped the Children's Aid Society to get money for poor children. He left at once to go to 25 North Street.

49

When he got there, he knocked on the door. A fat man opened it. He took Mr. Godfrey to a back room.

"Wait here," he said, and went away.

Mr. Godfrey saw a Hindoo book on the table. He began to look at it. His back was to the door.

All at once, he heard someone behind him. Before he could turn around, an arm went around his neck. He tried to get away. But he could not.

Something was tied over his eyes so he could not see. A cloth was put in his mouth so he could not call for help. Two men threw him to the floor and held him there. Another man looked in his pockets for something.

They did not find what they wanted. They grew very angry. Then they tied Mr. Godfrey to a chair. They left him there.

A long time went by. At last a woman opened the door. "Hello!" she called.

Mr. Godfrey made a noise with his chair. The woman came into the room and saw him. She took the cloth from his eyes and mouth. Then she took off the ropes that tied him.

"Who are you?" he asked.

"This is my house," she said. "I rent part of it. I rented it to a fat man for a week. He said he wanted it for three Hindoo friends."

"Where are they?" Mr. Godfrey cried, jumping up.

"Gone!" the lady said. "I saw them hurry away with the fat man."

"They got me to come here by a trick," Mr. Godfrey said. "I don't know why."

The things from his pockets were on the table. He looked and saw that nothing was missing.

"I don't know what is going on," he said. Then he went home.

But something else strange happened that day. We read this in the paper, too. Mr. Septimus Luker had also been to the bank that day. He had been to the same bank as Mr. Godfrey! When he got to his house, there was a note for him, too. It told him to go to a house on Court Road.

Mr. Luker went. And the same thing happened to him that had happened to Mr. Godfrey!

Just one thing was not the same. The men took a paper from Mr. Luker. It was a paper from the bank. It said that Mr. Luker had left a jewel at the bank. It said that no one could take it out but Mr. Luker.

What news! I was sure that the jewel at the bank was the Moonstone.

Miss Rachel wanted to see Mr. Godfrey right away. The minute he came to the house, she asked him what had happened.

"You have read the story in the paper," he said.

"I want to know more!" she cried. "I want to know about the three Hindoos. Are they the same ones who came to my birthday party?"

"Some people think so," said Mr. Godfrey. "But I could not see them. I know nothing."

"Do you know Mr. Luker?" she asked. "Have you ever met him?"

"Never," he said.

"Godfrey!" Miss Rachel cried. "Do people say the jewel Mr. Luker put in the bank is— the Moonstone?"

"There are people who say that," Mr. Godfrey said. "They do not know. And they should not say such things."

A strange look came across Miss Rachel's face. "Godfrey, what do people say about you?" she asked.

"Don't ask!" Mr. Godfrey cried.

"You must tell me!" cried Miss Rachel.

His face grew white. "Very well," he said. "People say that I took the diamond to Mr. Luker. They say he gave me money for it. They say I took your diamond."

Miss Rachel let out a cry. She jumped to her feet. "No!" she cried. "All this trouble is because of me. I have kept quiet too long!"

She turned to us. "Listen, all of you!" she cried. "I know who took the diamond. I know that Godfrey did not take it!"

Her mother turned very white. I did not know what to make of all we were hearing.

Miss Rachel turned to me. "Bring me a piece of paper," she said.

I did as she asked. She wrote on the paper: "I know who took the Moonstone diamond. It was not Mr. Godfrey."

She wrote her name after these words. Then she gave the paper to Mr. Godfrey. "There!" she cried. "Show that to the people who say you took my diamond. It will stop their talk."

She ran to her mother. "Oh, Mother, Mother!" she cried. "I should tell all I know now. But I can not! I can not!"

Miss Rachel ran from the room. Her mother looked sad. I did not know what to say.

Mr. Godfrey picked up the paper. "I can not let Rachel do this for me," he said. "People will think bad things about her. They will think she had something to do with taking the diamond."

"But what about you?" Lady Verinder asked.

"I do not matter," he said. Then he threw the paper into the fire. "Don't tell Miss Rachel what I have done," he said. "Let her think that she has helped me." Then he left the house.

What a good man, I thought, as he left. But what strange things we had heard this day! Miss Rachel knew who took the diamond. But she would not tell. Who could it be?

Could it be as Mr. Cuff had said? Had Miss Rachel taken her own diamond?

After Godfrey Ablewhite left, Lady Verinder called me. I went into her sitting room.

"I have something I must tell you," she said.

"Yes, Lady Verinder?" I asked.

She closed her eyes for a minute. Then she looked at me.

"Betteredge," she said, "you have been a good servant and a good friend. What I tell you now, you must not tell Miss Rachel."

"If you don't want me to, I will not," I said.

Then she told me that she was very sick. She had been told she would not live very long.

"Is there nothing that can be done?" I asked.

"Nothing," she said. "Do not be sad, Betteredge. But when I am gone, look after Miss Rachel as well as you have me." I said that I would.

Mr. Bruff, a lawyer, came that afternoon. He came to go over Lady Verinder's will.

It was late in the day when Mr. Bruff left the house. I was working in a little room next to the living room. I heard someone come into the living room. But I could not see who it was.

Then I heard someone say, "I will do it today!" It was Mr. Godfrey. He had come back and was in the living room. He was alone. He was talking to himself. But what was he going to do today?

Then, I heard Miss Rachel come into the living room. I went on with my work. Miss Rachel and Mr. Godfrey began to talk. I could hear what they were saying.

"Rachel," said Mr. Godfrey, "you know how I feel about you."

"You said you would not talk about that, Godfrey," she said.

"But I must," he said. "I think of you every minute. I care about nothing but you."

"Stop, Godfrey!" she said. "Don't say any more. Please go away."

But Mr. Godfrey would not go away. He kept on telling her how much he cared for her. He asked her to marry him. He talked for a long time. At last, she said she would marry him.

I heard them get up and start for the door. Then I heard a servant run into the living room.

"Miss Rachel!" she cried. "Please come at once. Lady Verinder . . . ." She did not finish her words.

With a cry, Miss Rachel ran from the room. Mr. Godfrey ran after her. I followed them. We ran to Lady Verinder's room. But it was too late. Miss Rachel's mother had died.

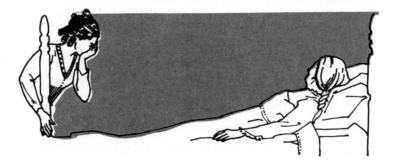

Sad days followed. Poor Miss Rachel was all alone in the world now. I did what I could for her.

Soon she and Mr. Godfrey will marry, I thought. I wished it were Mr. Franklin she was marrying. But I was glad she had someone.

The days went by. Miss Rachel grew very thin. She never smiled.

"You must eat more," I said. "You will get sick if you don't."

"I will try," she said.

Mr. Bruff, the lawyer, came to see her one day. "What you need is a walk," he said. "Come, let's go out."

They were gone quite a long time. The fresh air will do her good, I thought. She will feel better after the walk.

She was very quiet when they came back. I did not know what they had talked about. But Miss Rachel seemed to be thinking about something.

Mr. Bruff talked to her as he was leaving. "Are you sure, Rachel?" I heard him ask.

"I am sure," she answered.

Miss Rachel went to her room after Mr. Bruff left. She did not come down to dinner. I went to her room and knocked on the door.

"Can I get you anything?" I asked.

"No, thank you, Betteredge," she said.

It was late the next morning when I took breakfast to Miss Rachel. She was in her sitting room. She seemed to be deep in thought.

"I hope Mr. Bruff did not give you any bad news," I said.

"No, Betteredge," she said. "I was glad to hear what he told me."

"Then it must have been about Mr. Godfrey," I smiled.

She did not say a word for a minute. Then she looked up at me.

"*I shall never marry Mr. Godfrey!*" she cried.

"What?" I said.

"I shall not marry him," she said again.

"But I thought . . . ," I began.

"He will be here this afternoon," she said. "Wait until after that, Betteredge."

When Mr. Godfrey came, Miss Rachel took him into the living room. They were there a long time. Then Mr. Godfrey came out.

"Well, Betteredge," he said. "Do you know the news? Miss Rachel is not going to marry me."

"I know," I said.

He laughed. "Betteredge," he said, "I will tell you something. I am glad she feels that we should not get married. For weeks I have been thinking the same thing. But I could not tell her that, could I? Now she has let me go. And I am glad." With that, he left the house.

I could not believe my ears. He had lost a pretty girl like Miss Rachel and he was happy! What was the world coming to?

In a few hours, there was a knock at the front door.

What now, I thought, as I went to open the door.

There stood Godfrey Ablewhite's father! He marched right into the living room.

"What is this I have heard?" he said to Miss Rachel. "Is it true that you are not going to marry Godfrey?"

"It is true, Mr. Ablewhite," she said.

"Why?" he cried.

"I don't think we could be happy together," she said.

"What has Godfrey done?" his father asked.

"I have no more to say," she said.

"So!" he cried. "You do this to Godfrey. Then you have nothing to say! You think he is not good enough for you. Well, Rachel Verinder, I know a thing or two about you. I am glad Godfrey found out what kind of girl you are!" Then Mr. Ablewhite marched out of the house.

Without a word, Miss Rachel went up to her room.

What next, I thought. Can anything else happen to us?

8 Mr. Bruff's Story

Mr. Bruff, the lawyer, stopped in one day to see me. "Betteredge," he said, "you must wonder about all that has happened."

"Yes, I do," I said.

"I am going to tell you," he said. "A few weeks ago a friend told me this story. A man came to the London Courthouse and asked to see Lady Verinder's will.

"This news surprised me," Mr. Bruff said. "Who would want to see the will, I wondered. And why would they want to see it?

"I wanted to find out. I asked here and there. Soon I learned that the man's name was Skipp.

"I went to see him. I asked him why he had wanted to see the will. He did not want to tell me. But at last he did. He said another man had asked him to look at the will. This man wanted him to find out how Lady Verinder had left her money."

Mr. Bruff looked at me. "Betteredge," he said, "do you know who this other man was?"

"I can not guess," I said.

"Then I will tell you," he said. "The man was *Godfrey Ablewhite!*"

My mouth fell open. "Mr. Godfrey!" I cried. "Why would he do such a thing?"

"I will tell you that, too," Mr. Bruff said. "But first let me tell you about the will.

"Lady Verinder had quite a lot of money," he said. But she knew that she should not leave all her money to her daughter. She knew some man might try to marry Miss Rachel to get it."

"So what did Lady Verinder do?" I asked.

"She left Miss Rachel this house and the house in the country," he said. "And Rachel will have all the money she needs to live on. But no man can get his hands on that money. Even the man she marries could not get it."

"Good," I said.

"Now we come to Mr. Godfrey," Mr. Bruff went on. "I told you that he sent someone to see Lady Verinder's will."

"Yes. But why?" I asked.

"Mr. Godfrey needs money," Mr. Bruff said. "He needs a lot of money. He planned to get it by marrying Miss Rachel."

I saw it all now. Mr. Godfrey did not love Miss Rachel. He had only wanted her money!

"What did you do when you found this out?" I asked Mr. Bruff.

"I told Miss Rachel," he said. "That is why she told Mr. Godfrey she would not marry him."

"I am glad you found out in time!" I cried.

"I have another story to tell you," Mr. Bruff said.

"What is that?" I asked.

"Last week a man came to see me. He said that Mr. Septimus Luker had sent him. He was a very dark man. He was a Hindoo."

"A Hindoo!" I cried.

"He had a gold box with him," Mr. Bruff said. "He made believe he wanted me to lend him some money for it. He said he had asked

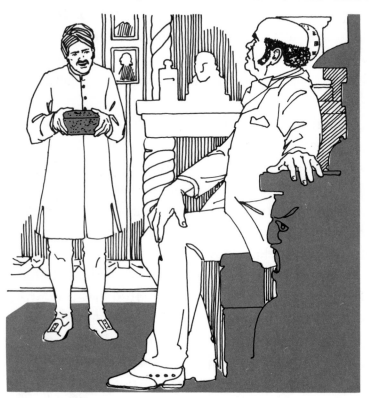

Mr. Luker. But Mr. Luker would not lend him any money. I told him I, too, would not lend him money.

"Then the Hindoo asked a strange thing. 'What if you had let me have the money,' he said. 'How much time would you give me to pay it back?'

"I told him one year. He asked nothing more. Now, Betteredge, what do you make of that?"

"I don't know," I said.

"I will tell you," Mr. Bruff said. "The Hindoo believes the Moonstone diamond is in the bank. He thinks Mr. Luker put it there. He believes Mr. Luker is lending someone money for it. So, he asked how much time a man would have to pay back money."

"Why?" I asked.

"Now he knows what day the Moonstone will be taken out of the bank." Mr. Luker will take it out one year after he put it there. I think the Hindoos will try to get it from him," said Mr. Bruff.

"That will be in June," I said. I remembered the piece in the paper about the jewel in the bank.

"Yes," said Mr. Bruff. "We will hear more of the Hindoos then. And who knows what other things we may hear!"

9 Rosanna's Letter

One morning, Miss Rachel was in her sitting room reading. I heard a knock at the front door. I went to the door and opened it.

There stood Mr. Franklin Blake!

"Mr. Franklin!" I cried. "I thought you were in France."

"I have just come back," he said. "Is Miss Rachel here?"

"I will see," I said.

I went to Miss Rachel's sitting room. Her eyes grew large when I told her Mr. Franklin was there. For a minute, she could not say a word. Then she told me to say she was not at home.

I had to do what she said. I went back and told Mr. Franklin.

He went away. But late in the afternoon, he came back. Again Miss Rachel told me to say she was not at home. This time he knew it was not true.

"Betteredge," he said, "she is still angry with me. I know it has something to do with the Moonstone. But I don't know what."

"If I knew, I would tell you," I said.

"I am going to find out," he said. "It might be the last thing I do. But I am going to find out who took the diamond!"

"How?" I asked.

"I am going to the house where Rachel's party was held," he said. "I am going to hunt until I find something."

"I will go with you," I said.

"But I don't want Miss Rachel to know."

"She will not know," I said. "As it happens, I have to go to the house, too. There are some things I must do there."

We got to the country house late the next day. It had been closed a long time. It did not look the same as it had when we were all happy there.

"Where shall we start?" Mr. Franklin asked.

All at once, I thought of something. "Limping Lucy!" I cried.

"What?" he asked.

"The girl who lives at the beach. She was a friend of Rosanna's. The day after you left, she came to the house. She had a letter for you."

"For me?" he asked.

"Yes. Rosanna sent it to her before she killed herself. She asked Limping Lucy to give it to you and no one else."

"How strange," Mr. Franklin said.

"I always thought Rosanna knew something

65

about the diamond," I said. "I think she wrote something in that letter."

"We must get it at once," Mr. Franklin said.

We went to Limping Lucy's house on the beach. She looked as wild as ever.

"Mr. Betteredge," she said, "who is this man?"

"Mr. Franklin Blake," I said.

She let out a wild cry. Before I could say a word, she ran from the room. She came back with a letter in her hand.

Mr. Franklin jumped up. "Please let me have it," he said.

She gave him a hard look. "You!" she cried. "You killed my friend. Take the letter and go. I never want to see you again."

Mr. Franklin took the letter. Then we left. As soon as we were outside, he opened it.

"Go to The Shivering Sand," it said. "Walk out on the rocks and lie down. Point a stick at the Beacon Lighthouse. Feel along the side of the rocks next to the stick. You will find a rope. Pull on the rope."

"We will find the box she hid!" I cried. "What will be in it?"

"We hurried to The Shivering Sand. Mr. Franklin lay down on the rocks. Then he pointed a stick at the Beacon Lighthouse. He felt along the rocks next to the stick.

"I have it!" he cried.

He pulled on the rope. Little by little, the box came up out of the quicksand. At last, he had it on the rocks.

Mr. Franklin opened the box. Inside there was a letter and a white shirt. He took them out.

"Look!" I cried, pointing to the shirt. There is a spot of paint. Do you remember what Mr.

Cuff said when the diamond was taken? He told us to find the spot of paint. Then we would know who took the diamond."

"But whose shirt is it?" Mr. Franklin asked.

"Look at the neck," I said. "The name may be in there."

Mr. Franklin looked. His face grew white. He stood as if he had been turned to stone.

"What is the matter?" I cried.

He handed me the shirt. I looked at the neck. I could not believe my eyes. The name I saw was *Franklin Blake!*

"You!" I cried.

"I did not take the diamond!" he answered.

"But there is paint on your shirt!" I said.

"I know nothing about it," he cried.

"Quick!" I said. "Read the letter."

It was a very long letter. In the first part, Rosanna told how she loved Mr. Franklin.

"You don't know," she said in the letter, "how much I love you.

"Then came the day the diamond was stolen. Mr. Cuff said the spot of paint would tell who took the diamond.

"I went to clean your room. I saw the paint on your shirt.

"What was I to do? I could not let them find out you had taken the diamond. I hid your shirt in my room. Then I went into town and got some cloth. I came back and went to my room. Then I made a new shirt for you. It was just like the one with the paint on it. I put the new shirt in your room. I thought no one would ever find out.

"I tried to tell you what I had done. But you would not talk to me.

"Then I knew what I would do. I would hide your shirt and this letter in The Shivering Sand. Then I would jump into The Shivering Sand, too. No one would ever learn that you had stolen the diamond."

Mr. Franklin had finished the letter. "But I know nothing about this!" he cried. "I don't know what to say or think."

"You did not go into Miss Rachel's sitting room that night?" I asked.

"I did not!" he said. "But there is the paint on my shirt."

"I will go to London," he went on. "I will see Mr. Bruff. He will help me."

Mr. Franklin went to London. I stayed on alone in the house. What was going to happen I wondered. How would we ever know if Mr. Franklin had taken the diamond.

10 Dr. Candy's Medicine

Mr. Franklin told his story to Mr. Bruff, the lawyer.

"Rosanna must have been out of her head," said Mr. Bruff.

"No, no!" Mr. Franklin said. "She wrote what she thought was true. It was that spot of paint. How did it get on my shirt? What shall I do?"

"Now listen to me," said Mr. Bruff. "We know the paint is on your shirt. But we do *not* know who was wearing the shirt."

Mr. Franklin's eyes grew bright. "Someone else might have had it on!" he cried.

"Or someone might have put the paint on your shirt," said Mr. Bruff. That is just what I think Rosanna did. Then she showed it to Miss Rachel."

"Why?" asked Mr. Franklin.

"So Miss Rachel would think you took the diamond," said Mr. Bruff. "Then Miss Rachel would never talk to you again. By doing this, Rosanna thought you would love her."

"What shall I do?" cried Mr. Franklin.

"First talk to Rachel," Mr. Bruff answered.

"She will not see me," said Mr. Franklin.

"I will take care of that," Mr. Bruff said. "Rachel will be at my house this afternoon. Go into the garden. One door in the living room opens into the garden. Rachel will be in the living room."

That afternoon Mr. Franklin went to Mr. Bruff's house. He walked into the garden. Then he went over to the door to the living room. Miss Rachel was sitting in the living room. She saw him as he opened the door. She jumped to her feet.

"Why have you come here?" she cried.

"I must talk to you," said Mr. Franklin.

"Why should I talk to you after what you have done?" she asked.

"What have I done?" Mr. Franklin asked.

"You ask *me* that?" she cried.

"Rachel," Mr. Franklin said, "I have come here to ask you something. Did Rosanna show you a spot of paint on my shirt?"

"No!" cried Rachel. "But you know how the paint got there!"

"I do not!" cried Mr. Franklin. "But I know you think I took your diamond."

"*Think!*" she cried. "I *saw* you take it with my own eyes!"

"You *saw* me?" he asked. "Rachel, I know nothing about taking the diamond."

71

She looked at him.

"It is true, he said. "Please help me. Tell me everything that happened from the time I left you that night. Tell me everything up to the time you saw me take the diamond."

"Very well," she said. "I went to bed. I could not sleep. So, I got up to get a book to read. I started to open the door to my sitting room."

"Then what?" Mr. Franklin asked.

"Must I tell you?" she asked.

"Yes," he said.

"I saw *you!*" Rachel cried.

"Could you see my face?" Mr. Franklin asked.

"Yes," Rachel answered. "Your eyes were very bright."

"Did you say anything to me?" he asked.

"No." she said. "I was afraid."

"What did I do?" asked Mr. Franklin.

"You went to the cabinet," said Rachel. "Then, you opened it up and took out the diamond."

"Then what did I do?" he asked.

"You stood next to the cabinet for a minute," she answered. "There was a strange look on your face. Then you left the room."

"Did you see me again that night?" Mr. Franklin asked.

"No," said Miss Rachel.

72

"And that is all you know?" Mr. Franklin asked.

"Yes," Miss Rachel answered.

"You should have said something the next day," said Mr. Franklin.

"And give you away?" she cried. "You took the diamond. I saw you. Now you say you know nothing about it!"

"And I don't!" Mr. Franklin cried. "I will show you that I did not take the diamond. Or I will never see you again!"

Mr. Franklin left the house and went to see Mr. Bruff again.

"What did Miss Rachel say?" Mr. Bruff asked.

"She said she saw me take the diamond," Mr. Franklin said.

"What?" said Mr. Bruff.

Mr. Franklin told him the story.

"I don't know what to make of it," Mr. Bruff said. He walked up and down the room. Then he turned to Mr. Franklin. "There is only one thing to do now," he said. "We must wait until the end of June. Then Mr. Luker will take the diamond out of the bank. The one who took the diamond from the cabinet will pick it up from him. But first, he must pay back the money Mr. Luker gave him.

"I will have Mr. Luker watched," Mr. Bruff

went on. "We will find out who he gives the diamond to. Then we will find our thief!"

"But I can not just sit and wait," said Mr. Franklin.

"What else can you do?" asked Mr. Bruff.

"I am going to find Mr. Cuff. He is the policeman from London who came to the house. I am going to talk to Godfrey Ablewhite, too. I may find out something."

Mr. Franklin went to Mr. Cuff's house first. But Mr. Cuff was out of town. Then he went to see Mr. Godfrey. But Mr. Godfrey had gone away, too.

Mr. Franklin had come back to the house in the country. He was very sad.

"What should I do now, Betteredge," he asked me.

"I don't know. But we must do something," I said.

Just then a man named Jennings came to the house. Jennings was old Dr. Candy's servant. He had something to tell Mr. Franklin.

"Dr. Candy was very sick after the birthday party," he said. "He died after being sick two weeks. He talked a lot when he was sick. He talked about you, Mr. Franklin."

"About me!" Mr. Franklin cried. "What did he say?"

"He was trying to tell me about something he had done to you," said Jennings.

"Was it about the diamond?" Mr. Franklin asked.

"No. It was something he did the night of the party," said Jennings.

"What?" Mr. Franklin asked.

"He said he had played a trick on you," Jennings went on. "He had someone put a strange kind of medicine in your drink. It makes you do strange things."

"The Moonstone!" I cried. "The medicine made you take the Moonstone!"

"Could it have done that?" Mr. Franklin asked.

"Yes," said Jennings.

"But I don't remember taking the diamond," Mr. Franklin said.

"You can not remember because of the medicine," Jennings said. "When you take it, you do strange things for a while. Then you fall asleep. I think that is what happened the night of the party. You took the medicine without knowing it. You were thinking about the diamond. You were so afraid the Hindoos would get it. The medicine began to work on you. You got out of bed. Then you went to Miss Rachel's sitting room and took the diamond."

"Why?" Mr. Franklin asked.

"You wanted to hide it," said Jennings.

"Then how did it get to London?" Mr. Franklin asked.

"I don't know," said Jennings. "But I think we can find out. We must make you take the diamond again."

"How can we do that?" Mr. Franklin asked.

"I will give you the same medicine again," Jennings said. "Then you will do just what you did the night of the party."

"And we will find out what I did with the diamond!" Mr. Franklin cried. "Let's do it at once."

"First, we must take care of this house," said Jennings. "It must look the same way it did the night of the party."

"We must ask Miss Rachel if we can do that," I said. "This is her house now."

"I can not ask her," said Mr. Franklin. "She would not even answer my letter."

"I will write to her," Jennings said.

"What if she will not let us?" Mr. Franklin asked.

"Then we will never know what happened to the diamond," said Jennings.

11 Watching Mr. Franklin

Jennings sent a letter to Miss Rachel. Soon her letter came back. She said we could do anything to the house we needed to. But she wanted to come the night Mr. Franklin took the medicine.

"Mr. Franklin must not see her before I give him the medicine," Jennings said. "My plan will not work if he does."

"We will not tell Mr. Franklin she is coming," I said. "I will send her a letter telling her to come to the back door. He will not see her."

"We must have some other people here, too," Jennings said. "I want them to see what happens so they will believe us."

We sent letters to Mr. Bruff and Mr. Cuff, asking them to come. We got everything ready.

Soon the time came to try our plan. Mr. Bruff and Mr. Cuff came to the house.

After dinner, Mr. Franklin went to his bedroom. It was almost 11. Jennings and I went to the kitchen. Soon we heard a knock at the door. It was Miss Rachel.

"Am I in time?" she asked.

"Yes," said Jennings.

"What shall I do?" she asked.

"Go to your bedroom," he said. "Be very quiet. We will bring the medicine there. You can watch me get it ready."

Jennings and I went to Mr. Franklin's room.

"When can we begin?" asked Mr. Franklin. "I am ready."

Jennings told him to lie down on the bed. Mr. Bruff and Mr. Cuff sat where Mr. Franklin could not see them.

"Now I will get the medicine ready," said Jennings. "Come with me, Betteredge. The rest of you must not move."

Jennings and I went to Miss Rachel's bedroom. Jennings took out the medicine and put some in a cup of water. Rachel wanted to be with us when we gave it to Mr. Franklin.

"No, Miss Rachel," said Jennings. "Stay in your bedroom. "Leave your door open a little the way it was the night of the party. Watch everything that happens."

Then Jennings took a stone from his pocket. He put it in the cabinet. "Mr. Franklin will think that is the diamond," he said.

We took the cup of medicine to Mr. Franklin. He began to drink it.

"Lie down now," Jennings said. "We will wait for the medicine to work."

The room was quiet. We all watched Mr. Franklin. In a few minutes, his eyes grew very bright. He began to talk.

"The Hindoos will take the diamond," he said. "I should have left it in the bank."

He sat up in bed. Then he lay down again.

"The Hindoos may be in the house right now!" he cried.

All at once he jumped up. "How can I sleep when I am thinking about the diamond!" he cried. "I am going to get it and hide it!"

He went down the hall. Jennings and I followed him. He went into Miss Rachel's sitting room. We hid behind the door and watched. I could see Miss Rachel watching from her bedroom.

Mr. Franklin went to the cabinet. He opened it up. Then he took out the stone Mr. Jennings had put there. He started out of the room. Then he stopped. He put his hand up to his head. His eyes began to close. The stone fell from his hand. Then he walked to a chair and sat down. In a minute, he was sound asleep.

We all ran into the room.

"It was just as you said!" Miss Rachel cried. "He took the diamond and was going to hide it. But the night of my party he did not go to sleep here. He went back to his room."

"The medicine worked too fast this time," Jennings said.

"But we still don't know what he did with the real diamond," I said.

"But we know he is not a thief!" Miss Rachel cried. She ran to Mr. Franklin and threw her arms around him.

Mr. Bruff and Mr. Cuff came into the sitting room. They saw what had happened. "We must find out what happened to the real diamond," I said to them. "Who took it from Mr. Franklin? Who took it to Mr. Luker? Who got the money for it?"

"On the last day of June," said Mr. Bruff, we will follow Mr. Luker. He will go to the bank. We will see the man he gives the diamond to. Then we will know who took it from Mr. Franklin. We will know who the real thief is."

12 The Luck of the Moonstone

On the last day of June, Mr. Franklin and I met with Mr. Bruff. Then, the three of us hurried off to the bank.

There were many people in the bank. Mr. Bruff pointed out two men.

"Those men work for me," he said. "They will follow the man Mr. Luker gives the diamond to."

A small boy came running up. He worked for Mr. Bruff, too. His name was Ted.

"I am watching!" cried Ted. Then he ran off again to hide by a table.

"That boy Ted is very quick," Mr. Bruff said. "He will not miss a thing."

"Look!" I said. "See the man who just came in? He looks like a Hindoo."

The man was very dark. He had black hair and a black beard. He was dressed in sailor clothes.

Just then Mr. Luker came in. He was walking very fast. He went to a back room of the bank. He was gone a long time. More and more people came into the bank. It was hard to see anything.

"Mr. Luker is coming back!" Mr. Franklin cried.

We watched Mr. Luker. He bumped into a man in a gray suit.

"He gave the diamond to that man," Mr. Franklin said. "One of your men should follow him."

Then Mr. Luker bumped into another man. "That may be the one he gave the diamond to!" I said.

"My other man will follow that man," Mr. Bruff said.

"Mr. Luker is trying to trick us," I said. "He is bumping into many people. We can not tell which one he gave the diamond to!"

"Where is Ted?" Mr. Bruff asked.

We looked, but we could not find Ted. We went back to Mr. Bruff's house and waited. Mr. Cuff met us there. After a while, Mr. Bruff's men came back. They had not followed the right people. It looked as though we had lost the diamond.

"Ted may have followed the right man," said Mr. Bruff.

We waited all morning and part of the afternoon. We were just about to leave when Ted came running in.

"What happened?" asked Mr. Bruff. "Did you see anything in the bank?"

"Yes," said Ted. "I saw Mr. Luker give something to another man. He was a dark man.

He had black hair and a black beard. He was dressed in sailor clothes. I followed him from the bank."

"Good boy!" cried Mr. Franklin. "What happened then?"

"Well," said Ted, "this sailor went to the Tower Wharf. The boats for Holland leave from there. He went on one of the boats. He told a man on the boat that he wanted to go to Holland. The man told him that the boat would leave the next morning. He told him to come back then.

"Then the sailor left the boat," Ted went on. "He kept looking around as he walked. He looked as though he were afraid of something.

"I kept following him," said Ted. "Then I saw something strange. Someone else was following him, too. There was a man on the other side of the street all the time.

"At last the sailor went into a place called the Wheel of Fortune Inn. He said he wanted a room for the night. In a loud voice, the landlord told him he could have Room 10. The sailor had a drink. Then, the landlord took him up to the room.

"After that," said Ted, "I came right back here to tell you everything."

"What happened to the other man who was following the sailor?" asked Mr. Bruff.

84

"I don't know," answered Ted. "He went into the Wheel of Fortune, too. But he was not there when I left."

"We must go to the Wheel of Fortune at once!" Mr. Cuff cried. "Hurry!"

We all left the house and hurried to the Wheel of Fortune.

"Take us to Room 10," Mr. Cuff told the landlord.

"That is the man who is giving me so much trouble!" cried the landlord. "A sailor took that room today. He said he was going to get some sleep. He asked me to wake him up for dinner. I tried to wake him. I knocked on his door again and again. But I have not heard a sound from the room."

"Quick!" cried Mr. Cuff. "We must break down the door."

Up we ran to Room 10. Mr. Cuff and Mr. Franklin banged at the door until it flew open. Then we all ran into the room. A man lay on the bed.

"It is the sailor!" cried Ted.

"He has been killed," said Mr. Cuff.

"How could that happen?" asked the landlord. "How could anyone get in?"

Mr. Cuff pointed to the window. It was open. "A man could get up on the roof," he said. "Then he could swing down through the window."

"That man who was following the sailor!" said Ted. "Do you think he . . . ."

"That man," said Mr. Cuff, "was working for the Hindoos."

"Look!" cried Ted. He held up a box he found on a table next to the bed. It was just big enough to hold the diamond. There was a note with it.

"This box belongs to Mr. Luker," the note read. "Only Mr. Luker may take it from the bank."

"But," I cried, "there is nothing in the box now."

"The diamond was in it," said Mr. Franklin. "And Mr. Luker gave it to the sailor."

"Who is the sailor?" I asked.

"Look!" Mr. Cuff said. He took hold of the sailor's black hair and pulled hard. The hair came off.

"It is not his real hair!" cried Ted.

Next Mr. Cuff took hold of the black beard and pulled it off. Then he took water and began to wash the sailor's face. All of the dark color came off.

"Godfrey Ablewhite!" I cried.

"Yes," said Mr. Cuff. "He is the one who took the diamond."

We stood there looking at Mr. Godfrey.

"Who killed him?" I asked.

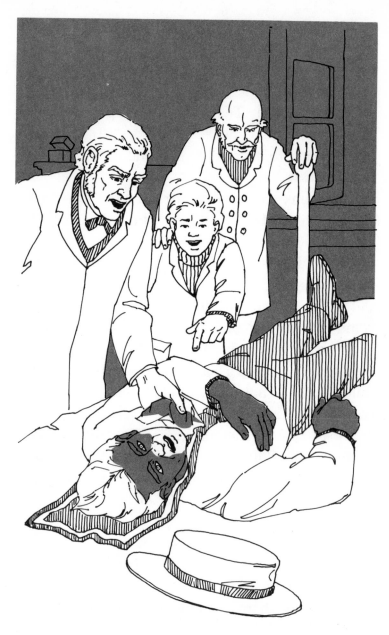

"The Hindoos," Mr. Cuff said. "They came in through the window and killed him. They took their diamond."

"But how did Godfrey get the diamond?" Mr. Franklin asked.

"We will have to ask Mr. Luker that," said Mr. Cuff. "He will know."

We went to Mr. Luker's house and told him what had happened.

"How did Godfrey Ablewhite get the diamond?" Mr. Cuff asked.

"He told me the story when he came here with the diamond," Mr. Luker said. "The night of the party he helped Dr. Candy play a trick on Franklin Blake. Dr. Candy gave Godfrey Ablewhite the medicine. And he put it in Franklin Blake's drink. Then he saw Mr. Blake take the diamond.

"Mr. Blake was going to hide the diamond in his own room. He wanted to keep the Hindoos from getting it. But the medicine put him to sleep. Godfrey Ablewhite took the diamond from him.

"He brought the diamond to me. He said he needed money. I gave him the money he needed. I held the diamond. I gave him one year to pay back the money. I would give him back the diamond when he brought me the money.

"The year went by. He got the money to pay me back. I was to give him the diamond at the bank. But he knew the Hindoos would try to get it. So, he told me he would be dressed like a sailor. He thought that the Hindoos would not know who he was.

"But they knew." Mr. Luker went on. "They had him followed. They found out how to get into his room. Then they killed him. They have their diamond now. They will take it back to India. They will put it back in the statue of the Moon God."

*   *   *

We heard nothing more about the Hindoos for a year or so. Then Miss Rachel, who was now Mrs. Franklin Blake, got a letter from Mr. Murthwaite. He was the man who knew so much about India.

"Not long ago," said the letter, "I was in India once again. I went to the city where the statue of the Moon God stands. The streets were full of happy people. I asked a Hindoo what was going on.

"He told me that they had the Moonstone. He said they were going to put it back where it belonged. They would put it between the eyes of the Moon God."

"I went up close to watch," the letter went on. "I saw three Hindoos walk up to the statue. They were the same three Hindoos I saw at your birthday party. One of them had something in his hands. He held it high over his head. It was the Moonstone!

"He put the diamond in its place between the eyes of the Moon God's statue. All of the people began to sing. They clapped their hands and sang: 'The Moonstone! The Moonstone! At last it is back!'

"I guess that is the end of the story of the Moonstone. It brought bad luck to many people. Many people have been killed because of it.

"But now it shines between the eyes of the Moon God. And as long as it stays there, no one has to be afraid."